MY MONEY CHOICES

YOUR MONEY

Claire Llewellyn

illustrated by Mike Gordon

WINDMILL BOOKS

Published in 2017 by **Windmill Books**,
an Imprint of Rosen Publishing
29 East 21st Street, New York, NY 10010

Text copyright © Claire Llewellyn
Illustrations copyright © Mike Gordon
Senior editor: Camilla Lloyd
Designer: Paul Cherrill
Digital Color: Carl Gordon

Cataloging-in-Publication Data
Names: Llewellyn, Claire.
Title: My money choices / Claire Llewellyn and Mike Gordon.
Description: New York : Windmill Books, 2017. | Series: Your money | Includes index.
Identifiers: ISBN 9781499481914 (pbk.) | ISBN 9781499481921 (library bound) |
    ISBN 9781508193081 (6 pack)
Subjects: LCSH: Money--Juvenile literature. | Finance, Personal--Juvenile literature.
Classification: LCC HG221.5 L56 2017 | DDC 332.4'9--dc23

Manufactured in the United States of America
CPSIA Compliance Information: Batch #BW17PK. For Further Information contact
Rosen Publishing, New York, New York at 1-800-237-9932.

MY MONEY CHOICES

Written by
Claire Llewellyn

Illustrated by
Mike Gordon

WINDMILL
BOOKS ™

What do you do when you
have some money?

5

We all make different choices.

I'd like a lollipop.

Some people have lots of money to spend.
They can buy almost everything they want ...

... even if they don't really need it.

If you don't have much money, you must spend it carefully. First, you buy the things that are really important.

Then what do you do with the money that's left?

You could spend it on the latest thing.

No. My old computer works OK, thanks.

You could spend all the money on yourself.

You could spend it on the people you love.

You could save your money for the future ...

... to help make your dreams come true.

You could give some of your money away
to people who need it more than you ...

... or to things you feel are important.

SAVE THE

WHALE

There are many different things
you can do with your money.

But only one person can decide what
to do, and that person is YOU!

Notes for Parents and Teachers

We all need to be able to manage our money and make financial decisions. The four books in the *Your Money* series are intended as a first step along this path. Based on children's everyday lives, the series is a lighthearted introduction to money, everyday financial transactions, planning and saving and financial choices.

My Money Choices examines how different people spend their money, according to their different financial circumstances, attitudes and values. It looks at the differences between "wants" and "needs" and explores the choices we make when we spend our money, and how these affect other people.

Suggested follow-up activities

• Cut out and price some pictures of things that children might buy with a dollar – for example, ice cream (50¢), candy (40¢), a bunch of flowers (60¢), a toy bracelet (45¢) or toy car (50¢) – and stick them on a piece of paper. Which one would the children choose? What would the children buy if they had to buy something for a friend, too?

• Cut out some pictures from a magazine of all sorts of things that children want and some of the things they need (e.g. shoes, paper, pencil, bed, cake, banana, fashionable bag or phone, snack, bike, hat, sunglasses, etc.). Talk through the differences between wants and needs. Then ask the children to look at the pictures and pick out which is which.

• Tell children to imagine they are going to start a new charity. Think about the cause they want to support. Think of a name for the charity. Then draw a poster for it, asking the children to help.

• There are many different charities. Which ones have the children heard of? Which ones do they think are the most important? Are they aware of national fundraising days, such as National Philanthropy Day? What could they do to raise money for them?

• Ask children to think about how they spend their money. Ask them to make a drawing of four different things they like to do with their money, and label them.

• Make a collection of pictures that feature things that are very important in life, things that are quite important and things that are less important. Stick them on a big piece of paper and talk about them with the children. Can they sort them out? Which do they think are the most important?

BOOKS TO READ

Learning About Money: Saving Money by Mary Firestone
  (First Fact Books, 2004)

Using Money by Rebecca Rissman (Heinemann Library, 2010)

WEBSITES

For web resources related to the subject of this book, go to:
www.windmillbooks.com/weblinks and select this book's title.

INDEX

choices 7, 21

dreams 17

generous 15
greedy 14

important causes 18, 19

money 4, 6, 10, 11, 14, 16, 20

saving 16
spending 5, 6, 8,
    10, 12, 13, 14, 15